PRAISE FOR BLACKWO
NEW BOC

"A golden key that opens a nev
— Jamie Sams, author *Earth Medi...*

"These words resonate deeply in my heart..."
— Walking Eagle, Spiritual leader and
Drug & Alcohol Counselor

"A profound blessing to all who receive it."
— Steven McFadden, Director of Wisdom
Conservancy, author *Profiles in Wisdom*

"Not only a book, but an experience."
— William H. Hodge, Ph.D., Anthropology

"Take the journey back to the ways of old in order to
return to Self."
— Phil Sidoff, M.A., M.S., C.A.C. III, Program
Coordinator, Limon Correctional Facility, Limon, CO

"To Blackwolf and Gina, I hold the highest respect for
sharing their insights and wisdom."
— Aught L. Coyhis, CACD III

"A great resource for healing and recovery."
— James D. Baker, M.D., Psychiatry

"A song of self, of community, and of the world..."
— Dee Sweet, Poet, White Earth, Anishinaabe

DEDICATION

To all the Healers.
Migwetch.

ACKNOWLEDGEMENTS

We would like to say Gitchi Migwetch to Caryn Lea Summers, RN, for gathering our thoughts onto these pages.

Commune-A-Key Publishing
P.O. Box 58637
Salt Lake City, UT 84158
Phone: 1-800-983-0600

Copyright 1995 © by Robert Blackwolf Jones and Gina Jones. *All rights reserved.* No part of this book may be reproduced in any form or by any electronic or mechanical means including information storage and retrieval systems—except in the case of brief quotations embodied in critical articles or reviews—without permission in writing from Commune-A-Key Publishing.

Library of Congress Cataloging-in-Publication Data
Jones, Blackwolf, 1935 -
    The healing drum / by Blackwolf Jones and Gina Jones; edited by
    Caryn L. Summers.
    p. cm.
    Includes bibliographical references and index.
    ISBN 1-881394-06-9 (pbk.): $9.95

    1. Self-actualization (Psychology)—Quotations, maxims, etc.
    2. Conduct of life—Quotations, maxims, etc.
    3. Mental healing— Miscellanea.
    I. Jones, Gina, 1960 - .
    II. Summers, Caryn L. (Caryn Lea)
    III. Title.
    BF637-S4J66 1995   299' . 7 — dc20
                                                    95-4182
                                                    CIP

Editorial: Caryn Summers
Cover design: Lightbourne Images, Ashland, OR
Page design: Quicksilver Productions, Mt. Shasta, CA

THE
HEALING DRUM

Blackwolf Jones, M.S., C.A.S.
and
Gina Jones

edited by
Caryn L. Summers, R.N.

This book is not intended to elaborate on Native American teachings or ceremonies. For those seekers wanting more, you are directed to find an individual teacher or lodge.

INTRODUCTION

by Caryn Summers, Editor

*"I dipped my paint brush in Blackwolf's colorful palette
and the beauty of Old Age wisdom effortlessly emerged
from each touch of my brush."*
— Gina Jones

While editing Blackwolf and Gina Jones' powerful first book, *Listen to the Drum*, I was moved by the poetic language in which Blackwolf's profound message was spoken. I found myself not only reading the words, but experiencing them. Here was a Native American healer who shared his sacred medicine with everyone —regardless of race, color or gender—in his own tongue, vulnerable and real. Here was a storyteller who could weave a story that felt as comforting as a shawl on a cold night.

I learned about tribal healing techniques:
• Mishomis are Grandfather Rocks that are used to release repressed emotions.
• Mitakuye-Oyasin tells how we are all related to each other and to the universe.
• Bimadisiwin helps us to find our unique purpose.

I explored the beauty of Earth, when Blackwolf advised, "Look at Earth Mother. All of Her birds sing. All of Her trees sway. All of Her waters splash. She carries Herself with grace and beauty. She lives with the strong heartbeat of Life."

I learned how essential we all are, no matter what our role or professional position may be, as Blackwolf asked, "Which wave is more important in the ocean? The big wave or the little wave? All are an integral part of the sea. For without the wave, there is no sea."

Blackwolf even taught me about humor the Indian way when he wrote, "Indians laugh a lot. Some laugh so hard that the chair they sit in shakes like a wet dog!"

Most importantly, I found my sacred connection and my importance on Earth when Blackwolf declared, "You are the connection between birth and death. You are the link between the past hoop and the forthcoming hoop."

May Blackwolf's words fill all of our days with wonder and with purpose, as we heal and grow together, "One Beat at a Time."

I am called Muka-day-way-maen'-gun.
I am Blackwolf.
In two worlds I have struggled.
I once experienced absence of Self,
and closed the door to the spiritual realm.
The door was pushed open by the Wind Spirits,
and I entered sobriety on March 30, 1977.
My story is not unlike others, yet it is unique,
as your life story is uniquely yours.

What is your struggle?

What is your conflict?

What are your chains?

I invite you to Listen to the Drum and be healed.

You will ride the currents of life,
as the eagle tips its wing
to feel the wonder of the sky.

invite you to stop...and listen.
I encourage you to attend...and listen.
I urge you to experience...

And listen.

In Indian, we say,
"How would a fish know it's
in water?"
The only way a fish would ever
   know it's in water
is if it were taken out of the water.

Take the time you need to give yourself the gift that the Universe offers.

Have you identified your pain?
Are you willing to acknowledge
that it takes a thorn to remove a thorn?
Healing is painful.
The thorn hurts as it enters the body,
but it also hurts when it exits the body.
The thorn begs for removal.
Realize your role as the healer
and remove the thorn.

Change is the silk of our cocoon. It is the garment we wear to the wedding of Self and the Spirit World.

To be Indian
is to hug a tree.

The tree has lessons for us.
Look beyond the branches' tips.
The branches reach out to honor Sky Father.
The roots penetrate into Earth Mother
for the gift of nourishment.
The trunk is the connector of energy
between Heaven and Earth.
The sap flows, manifesting life force.
Creator energy cycles itself.
The Spirit World has given us the opportunity
to learn from this truth.

The Spirit World works in harmony
with the laws of nature,
like the hummingbird that hitchhikes
on the back of the migrating goose.

Select a tree large enough to get a hugging grip.
And with soft eyes and silken touch, allow the connection to happen.
Ask the tree to strengthen you.
And thank the tree for sharing its energy.

Have you recognized the song of life as it sings through Tree's needles, leaves and boughs?
Trees have much to say if we listen.

The willow and the mighty oak stand side by side.
Along comes the wind storm and who remains?
The willow remains.
It was flexible enough to yield to tension.
It was rooted, centered and balanced.
This may be its greatest teaching to us.

When Fall comes,
　　the leaves display their carnival-colored
robes, like an Indian blanket.
The leaves teach us to yield to death and to die
　　gracefully.
For death is the ultimate life experience.

The autumn leaves are freed from their branches
by the Wind Spirits of change.
In rich color regalia, they dance their graceful
　　descent,
to blend with Sister Water and Mother Soil.
They form a fertile bed for Infant Seeds.

Can you see how acceptance of death
can compliment the hunger for survival?
Death is the survival of our spirit.

You are a gift from the Spirit World.

The Mouse teaches us concentration and focus.
If the Mouse is preoccupied or distracted,
it becomes vulnerable to the hawk's hunt.
Find the focus in your life.
Look up from time to time
or you may miss the most important lesson of all.

The Wolf teaches us endurance,
strategic planning and perseverance.
A Wolf can run like the wind or be as still
as a stone.
There is a time to be quiet like the stone,
and a time to actively pursue aspirations.
This is the Wolf's lesson to us.

Beavers teach about purpose.
Through endless chewing
and gnawing,
trees fall, dams and canals are built,
forests are changed forever.
Look to see what you can chew on.

The Indian does not
try to conquer nature.
The Indian flows with nature.

Joy is our pain
turned upside down,
inside out.

It is your responsibility —
your obligation —
to your Self and the Spirit World,
to become aware of all that is you.

The silence between
the beats
is where you hold hands
with the invisible.

Turn your wing tips into the current of the invisible and enjoy the possibilities of the winds of change.

Tune in and
hear the silence.
Now is for
the listening experience.

invite you to put your ear to the pulse,
the drum of creation,
and listen to the heartbeat of the Universe.
The space of silence between the beats
is where one finds respect.

We are spirits with bodies
rather that bodies with spirits.
Inside this scent of truth, old thoughts
reverse.
It is as though we have worn our clothes
of truth inside out,
and are now able to wear them as they
were meant to be.

We are breathed by the Great Spirit.
We do not breathe ourselves.
When the Great Spirit discontinues to breathe us,
we return back through the tunnel
to the Spirit World that we originated from.
Death is the giving of our breath
back to the One Breath of Life.

Earth Mother is the
source of nourishment.
Peace, serenity, and joy
are the fruits of Her blessing.
As we ground ourselves and
achieve balance,
we connect to Earth Mother.

Separating the fibers of Feather,
I noticed the spaces between.
Each opening had a story to tell,
for it had flown on the winds,
touched the currents of cold and heat,
of Cloud and Sun.
It had seen it all.

I wondered what the world looked like
from Feather's point of view.
What injury had caused the frayed edges?
What splendor did Feather see?
What music did Feather hear?
What invisible did Feather touch?

Experience Earth Mother.
Connect to Her.
Feel Her Pulse.
By doing so,
you will experience yourself.
You will reconnect to yourself.
You will feel your own pulse.

Consider a blade of grass.
Please, choose a blade from the many.
Get acquainted with it,
befriend your green-relative.
This is the only blade of grass
in the Universe exactly like it.

Nor are there two snowflakes,
nor granules of sand,
exactly alike.
Come to realize your uniqueness.
Understand that the Universe has chosen you
to exist out of an infinite amount of possibilities.

The Four Directions organize all
things.
They bring us the life cycles and keep
them renewed.
The Four Directions bring predictability
and order.
All cycles follow their form.

The color of the East direction is yellow.
The first rays of morning sun
bring the new light of innocence.
East is the white plumage of the Eagle feather.
It is the filling of the night container.
It is an infant.
It is the conception of a new day.
It is the spring of the year, stimulating new growth.
It is the creation of life.
This is East direction.

The color of the South direction is red,
the color of Earth Mother.
South represents summer and adolescence.
It is hormones exploding, experimentation,
and invigorating growth spurts.
Peer conformity replaces parental dominance.
It is a time for confusion, the precedence of
    wisdom.
It is a time to collect one's identity,
the time of the vision quest.
This is South direction.

The color of the West direction is black.
The sun trail takes us into the cavern
of Self.
We come to see Self in the deep, still waters
within.
The mirror of the Bear reflects our essence.
This is the autumn of our life, the adult years.
It is a time to bundle our knowledge into
wisdom.
It is time for us to empty our bucket,
so that we become filled.
This is to become mature.
This is West direction.

The color of the North direction is white.
It is a time for enlightenment,
a time to be purified and refined.
It is time to wear the white crown of Elder
    enlightenment.
From this spiritually dominant position
flows the eternal waters of life,
the wellspring of the life cycle.
The North contains shifting spiritual ice sheets
that move from great pressure.
A new spiritual construct results.
A Grand Canyon of Self emerges.
Darkness accents the light.
From the North all will be renewed.
This is North direction.

Beyond the Four Directions,
we are asked to go down,
to the fifth direction of Earth Mother.
The green color reminds us that
growth is needed.
Earth Mother supplies nourishment.
Earth Mother is our connection to life.

The Sixth Direction is Sky Father,
depicted with the color blue.
It reminds us to monitor our
life choices.
It is here where evaluation will
take place.
It is the connection to the world
from which we came
and to where we will go.

The Seventh Direction is you.
You are part of the hoop of life
that intersects Eternity.
This is the Direction to come to Self,
to recognize your role in life,
to give of your Self.

Chief Seattle said,
"Man did not weave
the web of life,
he is merely a strand in it.
Whatever he does to the web,
he does to himself."

Can you see that you and I
share the same breath,
and that by doing so,
we actually become one with
each other?

If I asked you to draw the moon,
what would it look like?
Many would draw the night moon as
    circular,
or crescent, and shining.
And that is fine.

However, ponder the truth of the moon as
    it reflects on the waters.
The shimmering light moving with the
    waves is just as real.
So is the day moon, invisible during the
    sun's time.
It is just as real as the nighttime view that
    everyone accepts.

It takes a soft eye,
like that of silk,
to open to the Spirit World.

It takes a hard eye,
like that of stone,
to see and be in the Physical World.

heard the song of Whippoorwill,
I sang it in my heart.
I wondered why it sang at night
the song of day's new start?

Prepare for the pain.
Prepare for the joy.
They are both your
companions.
Prepare for a new day.

Dare to feel the insanity. Paradoxically, this frees our sanity.

The experience of Self
is the permanent window to a
new life.
It is like the Sun's rays
touching the Earth for the first time,
the original rain falling and
beginning the cycle.
It is you laughing with the joy of life.

We all need to be recognized for the special person that we are.
We all need attention to nourish our child within.
We all need affection to heal our wounds.
We all need approval for our life choices.
All of these needs can be met by Self.

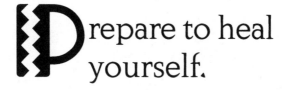

Prepare to heal yourself.

Beliefs beget values.
Values beget thoughts.
Thoughts beget emotional responses.
Emotional responses beget attitudes.
And attitudes beget behaviors and
    actions.

Deal with your monkey mind,
wandering wherever it wishes.
Take command of your inner thoughts.

Discipline your monkey mind.
You have your own mental rheostat.
Learn how to turn the lights on and off in
    your head.

You will be in charge of your thoughts
rather than your thoughts governing you.
When your mind wanders, bring it back to
    the task.

Prepare for disciplined change.

To come to know the world
    is to be wise.
To come to know oneself
    is to be enlightened.
To come to know the Universe
    is to be one with all.

Without the student,
there is no teacher.
Without the listening,
there is no message.

An Indian's wealth is measured
by what he gives away
rather than what he possesses.
This is the true meaning of Indian Giver.

What's the worst thing that will happen
if we become balanced, centered?
Will we become too happy?
Will we become too healthy?
Will we sleep too well?
Will we become too wise?
Too enlightened?

Don't miss the colors
and the dance of
the sunrise.
Can the sunrise be too beautiful?

Prepare for your
internal sunrise.
It is time.

Put your head on your pillow
and hear your blood flow
through your veins.
Listen to your Heartbeat.
Listen to your Drum.

The Medicine Man says,
"Hear your own heartbeat.
Put your ear to your own heart
and listen."

How was it that
you could not hear the messages
that were being sent to you each day,
through the beating of your own heart?
You could not see the things
that were in front of you each morning?
Feel the wonder that touched you each night?

Follow the fingers of the
　　Spirit World,
as they massage your entire
　　Being.

Mishomis, Grandfather Rock,
        has seen all,
        heard all, and
        understands all.
Mishomis has experienced all,
and understands all experience.

The spirit of Mishomis
knows your heart,
your fears, your pain,
and will help you find yourself.
Wearing his elegant robes of granite and gold,
the gentle Grandfather serves you.

Go inside, for that is where your home is. Ain-Dah-Ing.

The home within your heart
is where your Essence awaits.
Ain-dah-ing is this home.
Ain-dah-ing is a sanctuary of peace.
Here, you are safe
from the cares of the day.

Do not be in a hurry to get there.
For there is no "there."

Indeed, there are only "here's."
Stay with the now.

Cherish the experience.
Concentrate on the wonder of each moment.

It is like a journey into a beautiful landscape.
If you look only to the sunset, you may miss
    the sunrise.

In the silent space between the beats, you discover intuition.
Here is where knowledge freely flows.
Insights occur in the place of nothing.

Mash-ka-wisen means to be strong and accept help. The idea is to stand like a rock (be strong), and move like a river (accept help and be fluid).

You are the flower that
bows and cups itself,
a humble recipient of
Grandfather Sun's illumination.

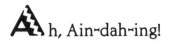

Ah, Ain-dah-ing!

Mash-ka-wisen is your gift to me.
I look from your view and I can see.
I open to your light and accept help.
You wash over me and I have peace.

Your energy moves through me and I am flexible.
I fill up with your power and I am without limits.
I drink of your splendor and I am strong.
I come to your silence and I am calm.

Ah, Ain-dah-ing!

The Medicine Man says,
"How can fear itself hurt you?"
The only way fear can hurt you is if
you react to it.
If you allow it to paralyze you,
it will become your master.

Either you will master fear or fear will master you. But there will be a master.

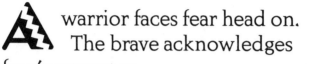

A warrior faces fear head on.
The brave acknowledges
fear's presence.
He considers options and alternatives,
and responds rather than reacts.
Fear is then neutralized
and becomes of no consequence.

The warrior says,
"If we don't face fear,
we will walk with it."

Fear is like poison.
It is good to know
poison's potential,
but it will not hurt you
if you do not partake of it.

Into the water's world she looked
To find where she belonged.
She found the answer staring back
It was her Self she found.

You heard my cry in the darkest night
And answered with your tear.
I wonder where our tears all fall?
Is their cup the ocean here?

Mitakuye~Oyasin means
we are all related.
This is the lifeblood of our existence.

I can not exist without you.
I can not exist without the Spirit World.
I can not be without the Great Pulse.

We are all related.
We are all connected.

The child in the womb
hears his mother's drum
keep a steady beat.
The old way was to bring the
    drum to the birth place.
The drum would sound steady,
    like Mother's heartbeat,
telling the baby that all is safe
    outside of the womb...
as it was inside.

When Indians hear the
   drumbeat at Powwow,
we come running.

Earth Mother's heartbeat
   makes our blood rush,
like her michi-zee-bee
   (greatest river).

Listen to your heart's vibration,
and you will connect to the
natural world.

Be present and listen to your pulse.

Walk to the pace of your own drum,
and you will hear a story about yourself.

Listen to the space between the beats.
The silence sustains each beat.
Like the strand that strings the beautiful pearls,
the Great Pause connects all of life.

Listen to the silence.
It will tell the story of where we came.
The story of where we go.
The story of the web of life.

Honor your fellow travelers.
See the divinity in all of them,
the yellow,
the red,
the black,
the white,
and the mixed.
All life is sacred.
See the image of
the Creator in one another.

Do not fail to see
that we are all
one within each other.

Listen to our Elders who say,
"When the bird dies, the song dies.
Then man dies, for he has no song."

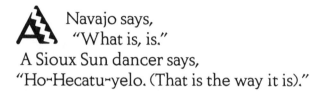 Navajo says,
"What is, is."
A Sioux Sun dancer says,
"Ho-Hecatu-yelo. (That is the way it is)."

Accept your relation, for that is the way it is.
Embrace your relation,
Hold hands with your relation,
for that is the way it is.

The Universe is a tree and we are her branches.
Give shade to your brothers,
and reach for the sunlight together.
That is the way it is.

Mitakuye-Oyasin means
we are all related.
I am your brother.
You are mine.
We are part of Earth Family.

Earth Mother loves her children,
from the fish to the birds,
from the blueberry to the oak,
from the ant to the panther.

From her seas to her mountains,
Both the weak and the strong,
the rich and the poor,
the young and the old.

cont'd ➤➤➤

➤➤➤ cont'd

With love and hate,
joy and pain,
life and death,
we are all related.

Yesterday, today,
and tomorrow.
Here and there,
we are all related.

Moccasin Mike said, "Respect all."
He respected the fly that circled his head,
and the horse that became his feet.
He understood that the extinction of the tiniest fly
brings loneliness into the souls of all directions,
for the Family is saddened when we lose a relative.

Abuse begets abuse,
    violence begets violence,
and respect begets respect.
Which way are we going?

Sitting Bull says, "If a man
    loses something
and goes back to look for it,
    he will find it."

We must return to the old ways
to find our lost treasures.

If my ax strikes Brother Tree,
what is My experience in that moment?
What is Brother Tree's experience in that
moment?
What is the Ax's experience in that
moment?
What is the Forest's experience in that
moment?
What is the Universe's experience in that
moment?
What is the Collective Experience in that
moment?
Every action emanates and vibrates with
repercussions.

Can you see we are one in each
    other?
We are of the same essence.
We are all born from Earth Mother
and will return to Earth Mother.

One of my favorite things to do
    is slide around in the mud barefooted.
I am simply dancing on myself!

We are made from mud and will return to mud,
for we are a fine mixture of Earth and Water.

Next time you get mud on your carpet,
    don't panic.
You're just looking in the mirror before
    your time!
Experience yourself!

You are the connection between birth and death.

You are the link between the past hoop and the forthcoming hoop.

Look up.
Learn from the clouds.
They are soft, yet
they have strength.

Wonder what the birds see
as they soar between the peaks...

See with Eagle's vision.
Hear with Wolf's ears.
Feel with Tree's branches.
Touch with Caterpillar's feet.
Smell with Bear's nose.

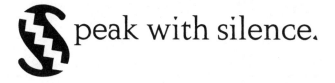 peak with silence.

Live life as your hoop
fades into ever-ness.

You will have these moments
to recall.

Imprint the now!

"Mine Moon!" the
   little one shouted,
for she understood the Circle.

We live on Circles,
we live beneath Circles,
we live in Circles.
Earth Mother and Grandmother Moon,
who give us our substance, are circular.
The Great Circle is the parental
guardian of all circles.

The Sacred Hoop is the Great Circle.
It circles the Source of All.
We follow its direction to become.

To return to health,
to return to life,
you must return to the Circle.

Thunderhoof

Into the Silence, I heard your thunder.
Beyond the horizon, I felt your beat.
Entering my heart, I knew your Spirit.
Thunderhoof, you have come for me.

My eyes were clear with anxious searching.
My ears were keen to hear your breath.
My arrow flew to meet your softness.
My voice called out to meet your death.

You fell and my heart paused to meet you.
You looked at me, I felt your pain.
You left your family and gave your Spirit.
Your tears joined mine in the misting rain.

cont'd ➤➤➤

➤➤➤ cont'd

See your robes warm my children.
See your bones prepare my food.
See your flesh become my body.
See how all of me is you.

Let your Spirit roam where I roam.
Let you recognize my call.
Let you hear my invitations.
Let you experience the joy of all.

Into the Silence, I will join your thunder.
Beyond the horizon, I will feel your beat.
Entering my heart, I know your Spirit.
Thunderhoof, you have danced with me.

An Elder closes the flap on his lodge in order to open the door to Ain-dah-ing.

The river empties so the buckets can fill.

Like the Council, listen with open ears.
Follow your path with honesty.
Fill your bucket with clear waters.
Speak with direct tongue.
Move with calm clouds.

On your journey in this life,
work to become truly open.

Allow others to see inside of you,
just as you allow your Self to see out.

Lower your defenses,
trust your responses.

You are present with what exists at this moment,
both inside and outside of you.

For, even on the Hoop of Life,
you are here in Ain-dah-ing.

Honesty follows the way of
   the hoop.
It is given and accepted and then
   returned in full circle.

Dare to see your Self as you are.
Dare to show your Self to those
   you meet.

Accept the pain that honesty
   must bring,
as well as the joy that flies on
   honesty's wings.

The flower,
     folded up at night,
looks at itself,
then shows its beauty
to the world in the day.

Speak with direct tongue.
Face what you must.
Do not run from fear,
nor push through it.

Commit to being open,
honest,
and clear
with your brothers and sisters.

Give yourself permission
to express your heart,
for Ain-dah-ing should not be
kept a secret.

Now is the time for minds to meet,
and spirits to join.

Without the mountain,
you cannot climb.

Without the climb,
there is no transcendence.

Without the transcendence,
there is no point in life.

Reflect on times in your life when
your bucket was empty.
Have you filled it with clear water?

Reflect on times in your life when your
bucket was full.
Have you emptied it?

Once you understand the dance,
you can empty your container of pain
and fill up with joy.

It's your bucket, you know.

To accept one's problems,
in the Indian way,
is to accept the sun's rising
and setting.

It just is.
It is part of life.
Accept.

Expect the sun to rise and set.
Expect the mountain to appear.
But only focus on the mountain when
   you meet it.
Only climb it when you must.
Only see it when it is there.

Gratitude is the greatest gift
you can give
on the journey of the Sacred Hoop.
It balances regret.

Say Migwetch.

The Medicine Wheel
is the Great Symbol for Life.
It is the center of all things.
From it all things flow.
It is the symbol of rebirth
and the origin of life.
Never ending.
Never beginning.

We become vulnerable like Brother Snake when we overextend ourselves.

We can only touch other beating hearts when we are balanced and centered.

Dandelion Song

I dance in Spring Wind.
I connect to Earth.
I open to Sun.
I reach out for Sky.
I stand now as One.
I dance in Spring Wind.

All is here for me to grow.
I remember you before me.
I dream of soft flight.
I move with the day.
I sleep with the night.
All is here for me to grow.

I dance in Spring Wind.
I wonder where I end.
I wonder where I start.
I am circled with my scent.
I belong and I am part.
I dance in Spring Wind.

As young children we danced with
dandelion joy.
We painted our faces with dandelion yellow.
Our parents were our view of the world,
our guidance, our validation.
We were ducklings following our mother's tail,
ready to offer our dandelion bouquets.

When you are empty of joy,
return to the East direction
and fill up with the wonder of childhood.

The Center of the Medicine Wheel
is Gitchi Manidoo.
The Great Spirit is eternal and does
not move.
It is the focal point, the axis, the
essence of life.
It is the unending presence of the now.

The eye of the Medicine Wheel
is as steady as the eye of the
Thunderbird,
the non-ending brightness of the Sun.
The eye of the Great Spirit holds
timelessness,
where memory of future and past
blend with the present.

Native Americans wear
the concept of time
like a loose blanket,
to be shed like the snake's skin,
if necessary.

Learn the lesson from Hawk.
    Visualize Brother Hawk
as he engages the poisonous snake —
    totally present,
rhythmically merging with the snake's
    supple moves,
mirroring the death dance of snake.

See the snake overextend himself with the strike.
Like a bull fighter using his cape to blind the bull,
watch Hawk use his wing to blind the snake.
His talons sink deeply to arrest the snake's strike.

This precise movement in the present
accomplishes a difficult task
through a vigilant series of small acts.
Inch by inch.
Moment by moment.
Learn from Hawk.

Catch the present,
  as the eagle catches
the fish.
Connect to the moment.
See what is happening now.

Without old age,
there is no
Sacred Hoop.
Without death,
there can be no life.

Notice how the wheel is balanced.
Remember your mind, your body,
your feelings, and your spirit.
Each is part of you, like the directions
   on the wheel.
Remember to keep it all in balance.

Feel Earth Mother awaken with
   new life in the Spring.
Hear the Wind Spirits singing the
   songs of change.
See how Birds fly as one with others.
Wonder why Brother Wolf can run so long.
Ask why Bear's tail is short.
Look to see why Beetle's wings are transparent.
Practice learning as Trees practice growing.
Cry with the Clouds' tears.
Laugh with the Flowers' dance of life.
Reach for the Stars.
Splash through the Puddles.
Remember the Mishomis.

Color your face with Dandelion.
Laugh along with Loon.
Sing with Vireo.
Set goals with Sun.
Reflect with Waters.
Stretch with Wind.
Work with Beaver.
Cry with Clouds.

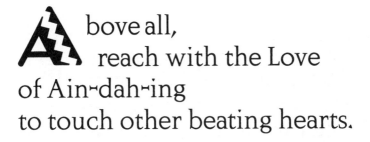

Above all,
　　reach with the Love
of Ain⁓dah⁓ing
to touch other beating hearts.

Brother Eagle soars just to soar,
As Running Deer must run.
Pine Tree reaches for the Light
Gifted by Grandfather Sun.

Medicine Bag,
       I place my heart
inside of you.

Know yourself.
Discipline yourself.
Be yourself.
Give of yourself.

Spend some time with
     yourself.
Get acquainted with yourself.
No distractions.
No excuses.

Find the courage to be yourself,
not a clone,
not an expectation.
Be uniquely yourself.
There is no one like you.

Remember
    what the Navajo says,
"What is, is."

A deer in the woods does not
    stare at the bear
and wish it were the bear.
It is fully content being itself.

You are responsible
to the Universe
to be who you are meant to be.

If you shake and shudder
at the thought of being who
you really are,
then shake and shudder!
You will not break.
Take the risk and flap your wings.
Be who you are!

The Indian way is "WE."
The women are in the center of the wheel.
They create and nurture life.
The men are at the periphery,
supporting the center.
All work together for the common "WE."

What is your talent?
Share it with others.
What is your strength?
Give it to others.
What is your passion?
Reveal it to others.
What is your understanding?
Teach it to others.

Chief Seattle taught
that man belongs to Earth.
Earth does not belong to Man.
Love the land
as the newborn child
loves his mother's heartbeat.

Return to the sound of
Earth Mother's heartbeat.
Notice how the sapling practices the
    whisper of its Parent Pine.
Hear the rehearsal of the eaglets' wings,
    learning to fly.
Listen to the water babble over pebbles,
as it trains itself to rush down the side
    of a mountain.

What does your heart practice?
What are you becoming?
Always, there are choices.
What you choose to practice,
you are choosing to become.
It is that simple.

Listen to the silence
between the beats.
Notice the is and the is not.
There are always two ways to look
at the same thing.
Your weaknesses can become
your strengths.
Your tears can become your joy.

Think of the Here and the There.
   You are free to move wherever you need,
to go wherever you must.

The path you are now on (Here),
will become only a memory (There)
as you travel to your next wigwam.

All pain, all suffering,
waits for time to take them There—
away from your Here.

Medicine Bag

I place my heart inside of you.
My love is nestled here.
I touch the stone that healed me.
I feel my mother near.

I place the gifts once given
Inside your soft embrace.
I feel the wings of Sparrow Hawk
Circle in my empty space.

I place my dreams inside of you.
My goals, my hopes, and fears.
I feel your power fill me.
I bless you with my tears.

I place myself inside of you,
My memories of days gone by.
I thank you for your opening.
You give me wings to fly.

The caterpillar does not say,
"If only I could fly."
It becomes and then flies.

The stone does not say,
"If only I could be soft."
It collapses into softness.

You, too, will fly.
You, too,
will collapse into softness.

The power is within you.

Bimadisiwin means to live life in the fullest sense—
to dance your dance,
your expression of Self.

Embrace Bimadisiwin.
Live fully.
Expand your ability to
    experience bliss.

Purpose is Life's yellow highlighter.

Listen to your heart as you run. It beats strong.

Your heart will provide the energy.
Your mind will provide the vision.
Your body will provide the vehicle.
Your spirit will provide the
    Mash-ka-wisen.

Learn the lesson of the acorn.

How does an acorn know to
   become an oak tree?
Because it yields to itself,
accepts itself,
so that it can become itself,
in order to experience itself.

Yield.
Accept.
Become.
Experience.

Remember,
   the mightiest oak
was once a nut.
There's an encouraging
   thought!

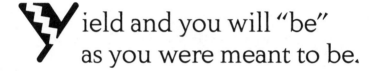

Yield and you will "be" as you were meant to be.

Be your truest Self and seek
your truest passion.
Find what pleases you.
Find what grabs you.

We are in harmony
with our purpose
when we experience an
inner state of joy.
This is our benchmark
and validation.

What is your joy?
What is your purpose?

Find it.
Confirm it.
Be it.
Then give it away.

Who's life are you trying
to live?
How can you live your life as
fully as possible?
What is your vision?

itchi Manidoo awaits to
guide your visions,
but you must choose to hear the
voice of the Spirit World.
You must choose to do what it
takes to fulfill your purpose.

The Creator
makes the change,
but you must be
willing to activate it.

Look for the rainbow in the puddle,
see the colors in the debris,
hear the symphony in your Spirit.

Then stir the puddle and watch the rainbow
reappear.
Separate the debris into a rainbow of color.
Sing a rainbow song within you.

Once you find ways to believe and practice,
you will become the rainbow.

At rippled edge of darkened Sky
Bows dignity of Cloud.
Colors honor Setting Sun
Moon and Stars are proud.

Sacred holds the dark and light,
Ant, and Hill and Hawks.
As fire splashes onto Her,
Respectfully She walks.

The highest of all Anishinaabe life principles is called Namaji:
Respect,
Honor,
Dignity,
and Pride.

Respect

Run your hands through the golden
    sands of time.
Each granule has a story, a purpose, a
    connection to the sea of Life.
Respect and see the sacred in all,
    the purpose of all,
    and the connectedness of all.
Feel the beauty of Life.
Experience the wonder of Life.
View the truth from different angles.
Let the granules fall through time
    and thank them for their moment.
As part of One, respect all.

Honor

Open up to life and experience life.
Life is your greatest fortune.
You are honored by all of Life.
Life gives you the sand to build your abode.
Honor Life by offering your best.
Build your life,
then let it sink back to Earth Mother and
    become part of Her.
Feel the welcome.
Watch how the sea of life moves your sands
    to their rightful place.
Honor all granules that touch you on
    your journey,
for they are your roots, your essence.

Dignity

Dignity is respect and honor for the Self.
Recognize your role in the sands of time
    and your dignity will grow.
Dignity is the headdress of Life,
    the blanket of honor and respect.
Dignity abides in the home within your heart,
    yet is connected to Earth Mother.
Connect and become a vital participant.
Give dignity to all and dignify all of Life.
Elevate the sacredness in all.
Dignity is not your achievement, it is the
    invisible support of it.

Pride

Pride is the sun's sparkle on the grains of sand.
Pride flows from the Sacred Essence
and provides the courage to protect your values.
Pride is the radiance of truth,
the joy of knowing yourself completely.
Pride is a gift you can give your children
as you teach them to build their own home
    within their heart.
Pride is connecting to the sea
that will wash your life back to its beginning.
Pride is embracing the circle of life.

All creation is equal.
Not man over snake,
nor snake over man.
All are one and one is all.

From the East Direction to the
North Direction,
the Children need the Elders
and the Elders need the Children.

Commit to all,
    become responsible
and accountable to all.

For all is committed,
responsible,
and accountable to you.

Namaji is a mutual Life principle.

The Red Road is the Sacred Path
between dark and bright.

Dark is the absence of light.
If we veer off into complete darkness,
Namaji demands accountability.

The glare of blinding Light
will cause us to veer off the Red Road,
causing us to become self-righteous and
   judgmental.

Follow the soft glow of the Eternal Light
and avoid the dark and bright sides.

What color is Brother Skunk?
    If you concentrate on the black stripe,
with a hard eye, Skunk is black.
If you concentrate on the white stripe, with a
    hard eye, Skunk is white.
If you concentrate on the whole Skunk, with a
    soft eye, Skunk is gray.

L ife is bitter-sweet.
    The blueberries my children
picked were both bitter and sweet.
The children left the woods not only with
    blueberry juice all over their faces,
but with dozens of wood ticks that
    accompanied the sweetness!

Walk in harmony.
　　Walk in beauty.
Don't cling to dark or bright.
Look for the rainbow in the puddle,
for every negative has within it a positive,
　　and vice versa.

Be deliberate with your choices and intentions.
Follow your heart.
Follow your dream beat.
Life is a boomerang and will return to you
what you send out into the Universe.

Softly place your moccasin on the Red Road
and you will find your joy.

Discover how Earth Mother's energy
supports you.

Walk gently on your Mother's Back
and she will embrace your step.

Honor Her and She will honor you.
Walk with Namaji down the Red Road of Life.

Manidoo is the word for spirit.
Gitchi Manidoo is the word for
Great Spirit.
Resist the temptation to define the Creator,
who is indefinable.
The more we try to capture the Creator's
essence,
the less we understand.

Perhaps you have experienced
the pleasing paralysis
a sunrise or sunset can bring.
This is a mere reflection of the
Great Spirit's awe.

We harmonize
with life by loving.

Look deep into the pool of the
other and see the Divine.
Look deep into the Universe and
see the Sacred.

Love is the essence of the
Great Spirit,
and the Sacred Mystery.
Love is the fountain of all creation.
Love Self and all of Life.

You are the creator and the recipient.
You are the potter and the vessel of the love experience.

Take this moment
and create the most pleasant
experience of your life!

Love is both a cause of
  greater health,
and an effect of greater health.
One begets the other.
But first there must be love.

Lie down on Earth Mother.
   Put your ear to Her ground.
Listen to the movement
that travels through Her.

Follow Her seasons.
Hear Her pulse slow with winter,
and quicken with spring.
Ride Her tides of timelessness.

Look up to Cloud Family.
　See the Clouds.
Watch as they race one another.
Observe their playfulness.

Follow their graceful dance.
Discover Cloud embrace.
Listen to their song.
Feel their spirits touch your eyes.

Fly with Cloud.
Know the ecstasy of sky soaring.
Time and space will be removed.
You will become one with Cousin Cloud.

Come to Blue Sky.
See its vastness.
Explore its boundaries.
Feel its open arms.

Blend in with its calm surrender.
Time and space will be removed.
You will become one with Blue Sky.

Come to the Waterfall for healing.
Cousin Water will wash your
negative emotions.
Let Waterfall's mist cleanse and empty you.
Cousin Water will fill you with positive
energies and vapors.

Come to the shore of a great lake or sea.
Sit and watch the waves.
See how they move in and out, like your breath.
Follow the movement.

Wonder what shores they have touched.
Imagine the stories of life that they carry.
Time and space will remove itself.
You will become one with Cousin Water.

Come to Cousin Fire.
Build a fire and watch the flames dance.
They will devour time and space
You will enter the Eternal Spirit World.

See how Cousin has two sides, just as we do.
The Dark side destroys and devours.
The Bright side can blind.
Look to the soft light.

Go back home momentarily and visit
your ancestors.
Befriend Cousin Fire.
It illuminates and keeps us warm.
You will become one with Cousin Fire.

Watch the clouds,
watch the waves,
watch the flames.
They take you home.
They take you to Ain-dah-ing.

Find a Tree.

Creator decided where the Tree should grow.
Thank it for giving shelter, and fuel for fires.

Thank it for giving cool summer shade
to rest the Elders and the sleeping Child.

Thank the Tree for giving its branches
for birds' nest.

Thank the Tree for giving its fiery maple leaf
to let us know when winter is near.

Thank the Tree for its running sap
that announces spring with its sweet medicine.

Thank the Tree.

Keep your eyes to Sky Father,
　　your feet on Earth Mother,
and send your prayers to Gitchi Manidoo.

Let the Eagle feather of your heart dignify
　　your gait.
Let the Great Drum give cadence to
　　Mitakuye-Oyasin.
Connect.

Become One.
Flow with the Great River of Love.
Namaji.

Do not take the Sacred Quiver away,
   for it contains
       his dreams,
         her songs
            and their dance.

Arrows need a source and a target.
You are the source, the bow.
The target is connection and separation—

Connection to Self and the Spirit World
as we separate from life's dramas,

Or separation from Self and the Spirit World
as we connect to life's problems.

I urge you to fill your quiver with straight arrows.
Empty your quiver of crooked arrows as soon as you realize what type of Arrows you are carrying.

Lighten up!
    Shed yourself and laugh!
The Creator must have a very good
    sense of humor
judging by some of His handiwork,
    including me!

Is there room for fun, humor, or laughter in your life?
Is your walk through life like plodding through slush and sludge?
Too much seriousness pulls energy and vision down.
People are as unhappy (or as happy) as they want to be.
What is your delight?

How happy or how unhappy are you? That is the question. You are the answer.

The arrow of anxiety
is fear
aimed into the future.

The mouse in the closet at night,
empowered by fear,
gets louder and louder,
bigger and bigger,
until it has grown into a ferocious bear.

Vines choke life
    from Brother Pine.
Creeping up the trunks so gracefully,
they are cunning and powerful.

Beware of attachments.
They can squeeze the life out of you.

Cut yourself loose from the vines that claim you.
Grow strong with your own roots.
Find the core of who you are and live with that.
Become that.
Let attachments fall to the ground.
Feel the freedom of yourself.
Breathe fully in knowing you are you.
Now you can grow, no longer stifled.
Be what life has asked of you.

Dependencies are driving forces that distract the person from an inner disturbance.

We cannot fly if we are attached
to our nest of familiarity.
We can never view the mountain
if we never take the risk
to soar on our own.

Judgments are egocentric
    condemnations of others
for their differences of views,
    actions, or attitudes.
ME is the point of reference,
    rather than WE.
The ME makes the rules to
    convict.
The ME prosecutes and judges.
The ME cuts the victim down,
in order to gain a false sense of
    control.

Judgment spreads like a lightning strike. Don't make others your lightning rod.

Which wave is more important
on the ocean?
The big wave or the little wave?
All are an integral part of the sea.
For without the wave, there is no sea.
Mitakuye-Oyasin.

Two little boys ran down to the sea
to experience the waves.

As the ocean retreated, they unknowingly walked
into the water's path.

And as the ocean returned to the shore,
each boy was hit by a large wave and knocked over
by its power.

The first little boy didn't want to get all wet and sandy.

He got up quickly, afraid of the power that had hit
him.

Coughing and spitting, he thought how terrible the
water tasted. Afraid, he ran away.

Seeing only the shadows, he ran to his mother.

Experiencing the wave as hostile, he hated the power
of the sea.

The other twin laughed as he got up from the wet sand.

He liked how his clothes felt, pressed wet against his
warm skin.

He smiled at the new experience of tasting salt water.

He was fascinated by the sea's power.

He waited in happy anticipation for the next wave to
cover him.

He loved the power of the sea.

If you let your Arrows of
    expectations fly,
you will be disappointed.
They seldom land where you
    had hoped.

The ice grip of Winter puts stress on
Earth Mother.
She acquiesces to Winter's claim, but she
is not claimed.
Her trees yield and the sap sinks down to
their roots.
Sink down to your roots and yield to the
stress of life.
Ground yourself to Earth Mother.
Root yourself in Ain-dah-ing.

Wear the world like
a loose blanket.

Look at Earth Mother.
　All of Her birds sing!
All of Her trees sway!
All of Her waters splash!
She carries Herself with grace
　and beauty!
She lives with the strong
　heartbeat of Life!

Come to Self

The first arrow in your Sacred Quiver
   is the arrow that comes to Self.
Travel your path to Self discovery.
Follow it to the deep pool of Ain-dah-ing.
Look into the water's mirror.
Realize your aliveness, your existence,
   your breath.
Look long and hard at your Self.
Walk the depths of your unconscious mind.
It will forever change your life experiences.

Befriend Self

Pull the second arrow from your Quiver.
Its target is the friendship of Self.
Are you in good or bad company when you
    are alone?
Befriend yourself,
your crooked side and your straight side,
your bright side and your shadow side.
How can you love someone you have not met?

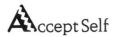ccept Self

Shoot forth the arrow of Self acceptance.
It is an arrow of tremendous energy
and guiding wisdom.

Appreciate Self

Feel the feathers on the Arrow of Appreciation.
Smooth them.
Come to value yourself, for you are unique.
You are valuable.
If you did not exist, the Universe would not be
    complete.
If the Universe was not complete, it may cease to
    exist.
You are that important!

As the snowflake has its
moment in time, so do you.
As a snowflake converts to water
and ultimately to vapor,
so will you eventually convert back
to Spirit Vapor.

Anger, resentment, guilt and remorse freeze the flower in you and prevent it from blossoming.

We spend our entire lifetime in our body,
day and night, asleep and awake,
at home, at work, at play.
And for this intimate experience,
do we love ourselves?
Have we come to see our sacred light?
Have we come to Ain-dah-ing?

Thank your fingers for protecting you.
Thank your toes and feet for bearing your weight
and carrying you great distances down your path of life.
Thank your heart for maintaining a constant beat
which pumps your blood throughout your body.
Thank your arteries and veins for being rivers and
streams that carry nourishment and breath to your
internal encampments.
Thank your nose for bringing you all the pleasurable scents
that are found in the forest.
Thank your eyes for beholding the beauty of the sunset.
Thank your skin for being your rain coat in the storm.
Thank your ears for helping you hear the symphony of
the Universe.
Thank your tongue for giving your parched throat the
experience of a cool fresh drink of water, the
beverage of the Creator.

Anishinaabe Prayer

How then can I tell you of my love?
Strong as the Eagle, Soft as the Dove.
Patient as the Pine Tree that stands in the sun.
And whispers to the wind, "You are the One."

The first questions the Creator
might ask when we return home
to the Spirit World is,
"Did you enjoy my creation?
Did you bask in the sun?
Did you listen to the bird singers?
Did you smell Sister Cedar's perfume?
Did you see the glistening dew polish
    Cousin Fern?
Did you taste the fruit of the forest?"

Look to Life to provide joy
and happiness.
Wear the joy well with your
laugh and smile lines.

Your face
   is the billboard
of your lifestyle.

Indians laugh a lot.
Some laugh so hard
that the chair they sit in
shakes like a wet dog!

Humor is no more than contradiction, and life is filled with it!

We are here for such a short time, so enjoy the experience!

Give your time, your Self, to others.
Help with a door,
slow down for the aged,
read to a child.
Give your best.
Share your smiles.
Share your joy
as well as your sadness.
Serve others to serve yourself.
That is integrity.

If you think you are humble,
you probably are not.
If you think you're not humble,
you probably are.

Practice humility, for humility
opens the door to patience.
Practice patience, for patience opens
the door to tolerance.
Practice tolerance, for tolerance opens
the door to compassion.
Practice compassion for it swings back
open to humility.
Reach within yourself to enrich society.
Enrich society and you will enrich
yourself.
Practice all of these aspects of Self and
you will know integrity.

Woman has within her
the soft secret of creation,
as all things are born from her.
She is the center of society.

The male's hard conceptive seed
pierces the soft female egg,
just as Acorn pierces Mother Earth.

When these two energies combine,
the two produce the One.

What is emptied
is filled,
(conception)
and what is filled
is emptied
(birth).

See with soft focus.
Create and nurture.
See the Spirit World with soft eyes
and give it form.

See with hard focus.
Initiate and support.
See the Physical World with hard
eyes and give it honor.

Only the person carrying the Quiver knows of the purpose, knows of the vision.

It is the sacred right of the traveler to follow his own vision, to follow her path on the Sacred Hoop of Life.

Do not take the Sacred Quiver away from him, for it contains his dreams, her songs and their dance.

Do not discount the size of his quiver, for you do not know the threads that it is made of.

Wear bells and jingles and
celebrate life movements!
Let the jingles encourage the spirits to
dance with you,
especially your spiritual animal affinity.

O Great Spirit,
whose voice I hear in the winds,
and whose breath gives life to all the world,
hear me! I am small and weak.
I need your strength and wisdom.

Let me walk in Beauty and make my eyes ever
behold the red and purple sunset.
Make my hands respect the things you have made
and my ears sharp to hear your voice.
Make me wise so that I may understand
the things you have taught my people.
Let me learn the lessons you have hidden
in every leaf and rock.

cont'd ➤➤➤

►►► cont'd

I seek strength
Not to be greater than my brother,
but to fight my greatest enemy — myself.
Make me always ready to come
to you with clean hands and straight eyes,
so when life fades, as the fading sunset,
my spirit may come to you without shame.

Mitakuye-Oyasin

(prayer read at Indian Alcoholics Anonymous meetings)

A mother's heartbeat is the song of her child,
connecting her child to the world.
You are Earth Mother's child.
Hear Her vibration and connect to
    Her pulse,
for the Drum speaks through Her
    to those who listen.

Hear the water drums' soft beat.
Hear the strong beat of Powwow.
Sound your own distinct drum and
   join the Great Pulse of all.
No drum is too small,
No beat is too soft.
All contribute.
Participate joyfully with the great
   vibration of the Universe.
Dance to your own rhythm and
   celebrate your life.

Don't worry,
Don't hurry,
Do your best,
and forget the rest!

The Drum is steady,
always in the Now.
Each beat is as important
as the one before and the
one to follow.

Worry is like taking a blank sheet of paper,
placing it on your mind's easel,
and drawing a horrible fairy tale.
Your animated horror causes panic.
Unable to distinguish between pretend and real,
you become the victim of your own imagination.

Since all worry is in the future,
all you need to do is switch
back to the present.
If you find yourself in future,
turn off your worry switch and
   live in the Now.

The Great Drum is steady
and maintains the beat of Life.
There is no rush.

Slow down.
    Come to Self.
Come to Ain-dah-ing.
Drink the sweet waters of your
    Inner Spring.

Each moment is worthy of a full pulse.
Don't hurry.
You were not made to hurry.
Hurry is an effort to distract from Self.
Distraction prevents us from accessing
Ain-dah-ing.
Your home within your heart
houses your tranquillity.
The more you hurry,
the further away you get from home.
The further you get from home,
the more you feel empty inside.
If this emptiness is not filled internally,
it will seek fulfillment externally.
The door is left wide open for addiction,
or the erosion of identity.

Do your best and you will have done your best.

In the sacred Midewinin Eagle
Medicine Lodge,
the Medicine Man makes a mistake
in his elaborate beadwork
to announce his humanity.
This obvious mistake reveals that
    all are flawed,
that no one is exempt.

Let go of trying to control people, places and things. You can't anyway, so why try?

Lift your head.
    Look up.
Respect all.
Fear none.
And let the Spirit World
    take care of the rest.

Children are the fabric
   of our future.
Honor them.
Do nothing which shall
   harm them.

If we live in harmony with the Child of All,
the Sky is clear, the Earth is solid.
All is content, flourishes,
and the sacred cycle renews.
When the Child within all is abused,
the Sky becomes dirty, and the Earth barren.
Balance is lost and creatures disappear forever.

Your greatest treasure is your Child within.
Continue to nurture your Child even
as you grow old.
This Child is forever a part of you.
The Child within gifts you
    the freedom that you crave,
    the spontaneity you wish for,
    the wonder you desire.
Go to the East direction when in need of
    these things.
Remain connected to your Child within.

See with Child eyes and you will see the affinity of life.

Children are our riches.
View the children in different lights,
like a beautiful stone with many facets.
Allow them the freedom to be a child,
yet bless them with limits and boundaries.
For that is nourishment for their shell.

We are all moving along the River of Life.
Enjoy the scenery.
Look and you will see the Creator.
Fish along the way and play.
Pull your canoe up on the shoreline and rest.
Pick berries and collect them in your birch bark basket.
Taste the blueberry, and you will taste the Creator.
Build a nice fire and cook your fish.
Taste the fish and you will taste the Creator.
Burn cedar, sage and sweet grass.
You will smell the Creator.
Place tobacco down and thank the Four Directions for
    their gifts.
Watch the Sun trail to the West.
It is the glory of the Creator.
Tell your companions of your journey and listen to theirs.
Tell stories around the fire and enjoy each other's
    company.
Tell jokes. Laugh. Enjoy.
Look into the eternity of Cousin Fire
    and you will touch the Creator's Pulse.
Rest under Grandmother Moon's gaze and sleep well.

All rivers lead to the Ocean.
All streams lead to the Creator.
Mitakuye Oyasin.
We are all related.

You are two-thirds water
and one-third earth.
Pray with your internal water
drum to the Spirit World.
The water drum represents
the merging of Earth and
the spiritual dimensions.
Send your beat to the Creator
from your water drum.

Have faith in the one you love
and the one who loves you —
the Creator.

Your tongue is to speak with
when you know what to say
and how to say it.

Your teeth are to keep your
tongue in your mouth
until you figure it out.

May your Prayers
fly on the wings
of Brother Eagle.

Meditation begins where thought ends.

Listen to the unseen voices,
  Peepers in the spring,
Birds high above,
snapping Twigs,
Brother Chipmunk.

Look up to Grandfather Sun,
    Grandmother Moon,
Cousin Cloud and all the Star people.
They sing and dance the song of the
    Universe.
They speak to your heart.

Sky Drum resonates throughout the
    Universe.
Sky Drum's vibrations make the stars
    flicker.
Grandmother Moon casts Her shadow
down on the great waters, making the
    tides flow.

cont'd ➤➤➤

▶▶▶ cont'd

Dance to Sky Drum.
Celebrate with the Night Singers.
Join Brother Wolf and
   Sister Whippoorwill
as they provide a chorus from
   here below.

As you look up with appreciation,
   Sky family looks down,
as Grandparents watching their
   grandchildren frolic.
The old need the young and the
   young need the old.
Sky needs you, as you need the Sky.

Mitakuye-Oyasin.

Learn from Turtle.

Turtle rests on a log, stops its life, quiets,
and basks in Grandfather Sun's rays.
Turtle sheds the leeches that cling to its shell.

Stop your life, quiet to meditation,
and open to the Great Spirit's White Light.
Shed the stresses and tensions that cling to
    your shell.

Quiet the noise of your Self
and rest your head on the
pillow of life.
Listen and you will hear the
Pulse of the Creator.

Celebrate your own mystery by exploring your spiritual caves and caverns.

Come to the center of your existence,
    your well-spring within,
where the voices of your Grandfathers and
    Grandmothers murmur.
This is the center of your heart, the alignment
    of your mind, body, and spirit.
It is the space between the tricksters of desire
    and fear.
Here you will not be distracted from Self.

Listen to the voice
  of the Great Spirit
in your heartbeat.
Come to the center of your
  existence and listen.

My eyes followed the sacred smoke trail
into Sky Father.
I watched as four eagles flew in from each
direction.
Soaring on Cousin Wind, they neared each other.
Meeting as brothers, they became a great hoop
above us.
And connecting to the beat of the eternal,
I said, "Ah ho."

GLOSSARY

Word	Pronunciation	Definition
Ain-dah-ing	AH-da-ning	Home within our heart.
Anishinaabe	a-ni-shi-NA-bae	The ancestors of the Ottawa, Potawatomi, and Ojibway tribes.
Bimadisiwin	be-ma-DEE-zee-win	To live life to the fullest. To become and fulfill one's fate and purpose. To engage free will. Sometimes spoken by elders to mean: to live the good life.
Boo-zhoo	Bou-zshoo	Hello.
Cedar medicine		Used in many spiritual ceremonies to provide a channel to the Spirit World.
Crooked Arrows		Arrows that will bring you to greater pain.
Eagle Medicine Feather		Known in Ojibwa tradition to be used in healings.
Earth Mother		The female, creative, nurturing qualities of Earth.
Four Directions		The Directions of the medicine wheel: East, South, West and North.
Gitchi	GI-chi	Great.
Gitchi Manidoo	GI-chi MON-ee-doo	Great Spirit.

Gitchi Migwetch	GI-chi ME-gwich	Big thank you.
Kinnikinnick	KIN-ee-kin-ik	"Much mixed." Is a tobacco based mixture also accompanied with other herbs, primarily: cedar, balsam fir, sweet grass, calamus root, sweet non-fern, sweet gale and mints. Other mixtures may also include bear berry, sweet goldenrod, rose petals, sage, willow bark, red ooshier bark, sweet clover yarrow and tobacco. Used in Native American sacred ceremonies.
Manidoo	MON-ee-doo	Spirit.
Mash-ka-wisen	mash-KOW-sin	Inner strength.
Medicine Bag		A Native American healing pouch that contains a variety of herbs, medicines etc. used to connect the participant to the Spiritual Realm.
Medicine Wheel		A Native American healing wheel to represent balance in one's life, as well as a symbol for life cycles. The Medicine Wheel has three parts: the circumference (the Sacred Hoop), the center (Gitchi Manidoo), and the Four Directions (East, South, West, and North).

Word	Pronunciation	Definition
Michi-Gami	MICH-ee-GAM-ee	Great water. The root word of Michigan.
Midewinin	mi-DAY-win	Sacred Medicine lodge of the Ojibway people.
Migwetch	ME-gwich	Thank you.
Mishomis	mi-SHOO-mis	Grandfather in the Ojibway language. A term for the spiritual healing stone.
Mitakuye-Oyasin	mi-TAHK-wee-a-say	We are all related.
Mu-kwa	MA-kwa	Bear
Namaji	NA-MA-GEE	The highest Anishinaabe principle: respect, honor, dignity and pride.
Nokomis	No-KO-mis	Grandmother.
Prayer Stick		A way to lift your prayers to the Great Spirit.
Red Road		The guiding principle to stay between virtue and evil, to have a positive focus.
Sacred Hoop		A Native American symbol for our journey in this life, our connection to the Spirit World. The cycle of all things.
Sacred Quiver		The container for sacred arrows (guiding principles) to live by.
Sahgeen	San-GEEN	Love and respect.

Seven Directions	The seven directions for one's life: East to the eagle, South to the wolf, West to the buffalo, North to the bear, into Earth Mother, out to Sky Father and yourself—the seventh direction.
Shape Shift	A cognitive reframing.
Sky Father	Recognizing the conceptual, supportive qualities of Sky.
Straight Arrows	Principles that will bring you to greater health and connection with the Universe.
Vision Quest	A Native American ceremony where the participant abstains from food, light, etc. in order to obtain a spiritual vision to guide his free will in directing his purpose. Sometimes conducted in pits, mountain tops, or near a waterfall.

INDEX

ABOUT THE AUTHORS

Muka-day-way-ma-en'-gun, Blackwolf, is the Indian name given to co-author Robert Jones. He is of Ojibway heritage and lived on the Lac Courte Oreilles -Ojibway reservation during his formative years. Blackwolf frequently visits his home to renew and further the Anishinaabe way.

Blackwolf achieved sobriety in 1977 within the fellowship of Alcoholics Anonymous and has enjoyed continuous sobriety since that time. He holds a Bachelor's degree in Psychology, a Master's degree in Guidance and Counseling and has accomplished post graduate studies in Addictive Disorders. He is a licensed psychotherapist, a Certified Addiction Specialist, and has published in an international professional journal. He maintains a private clinical practice and speaks nationally on using Native American healing techniques within the psychotherapeutic process.

Gina Jones is of Mohawk ancestry. She, too, has enjoyed continuous sobriety since 1979. Holding a Bachelor's of Science degree in Education, Gina is presently a sixth grade teacher. She presents inservice training on Reading and Writing Workshops for educators in Wisconsin.

Gina writes in her free time on her own projects, as well as in conjunction with her husband. She has published curriculum material through CESA (Cooperative Educational Service Agency) in Wisconsin, poetry in literary publications, and is currently looking forward to publishing other material, including children's books and young adult novels.

OTHER COMMUNE-A-KEY PRODUCTS

Caregiver, Caretaker: From Dysfunctional to Authentic Service in Nursing.
by Caryn Summers. Essential reading for helpers who tend to care for others
before caring for themselves. $16.95 each.

Inspirations for Caregivers. A classic selection of inspirational quotes
collected by Caryn Summers on the motives and rewards for giving care to
others. $9.95 each.

Inspirations for Caregivers: Music and Thoughts. Caryn Summers reads the
best quotes from *Inspirations for Caregivers,* accompanied by original music by
Douglas York. $10.95 each.

Circle of Health: Recovery Through the Medicine Wheel. by Caryn Summers.
This personal growth book combines mythology, symbols, Native American
tradition and psychology with twelve-step recovery tools. $12.95 each.

the Girl, the Rock and the Water. by Caryn Summers. A mythological journey
of our inner child to safety, trust and freedom. Includes watercolor illustrations,
audio soundtrack read by the author, and workbook. $19.95 each.

Heart, Humor & Healing. by Patty Wooten, RN. A delightful collection of
inspiring, fun-filled and laughter provoking quotes designed to promote healing
in the patient as well as the caregiver. $9.95 each.

Listen to the Drum: Blackwolf Shares his Medicine. by Blackwolf Jones and
Gina Jones. Return to "old age wisdom" as Blackwolf offers healing techniques
from the ancients of Native America. For both Indian and non-Indian audiences.
                                                                    $12.95 each.

The Healing Drum. by Blackwolf Jones and Gina Jones. The poetic thoughts
imparted in *Listen to the Drum* are beautifully expressed in this gift book. Hear the
message of self-help, "One beat at a time." $9.95 each.

ORDER FORM

Need copies for your friend? You may find books published by Commune-A-Key at your local bookstore or you may order directly.

TITLE	QTY	TOTAL
Caregiver, Caretaker: From Dysfunctional to Authentic Service in Nursing. $16.95 each.		
Inspirations for Caregivers. $9.95 each.		
Inspirations for Caregivers: Music and Thoughts. $10.95 each.		
Circle of Health: Recovery Through the Medicine Wheel. $12.95 each.		
the Girl, the Rock and the Water. $19.95 each.		
Heart, Humor & Healing. $9.95 each.		
Listen to the Drum. $12.95 each.		
The Healing Drum. $9.95 each.		

Mail this form with your check or money order payable to:
Commune-A-Key Publishing
P.O. Box 58637
Salt Lake City, UT 84158
1-800-983-0600

SUBTOTAL _____

Shipping & handling: $3.50 first item, plus $1.25 each additional item. _____

TOTAL $ ENCLOSED _____

Name _____ Phone _____

Address _____

City _____ State _____ Zip _____